Embroidery is an art that has been cherished for centuries, and it always brings joy to create something beautiful with needle and thread. One of the most important aspects of embroidery is finding the perfect color palette, which can be a daunting task for beginners and experienced crafters.

Our 100-color palette, inspired by the seasons, offers endless possibilities for creating stunning embroidery designs that capture the essence and mood of each season.

Who is this book for?

- **For both beginner and experienced embroiderers** who seek color inspiration for their embroidery projects or need to substitute colors on a pre-made pattern. If you've bought an embroidery pattern that features colors you don't quite like, or if you're seeking inspiration for your embroidery, this book is perfect for you. It offers valuable assistance to anyone struggling to create harmonious thread color combinations.

- **For those who design patterns**, these color palettes can be an excellent resource to produce stunning and cohesive embroidery designs that draw inspiration from nature, wildlife, people, everyday objects, and situations. Using these palettes can help you produce embroidery designs that are both balanced and coherent. Simply draw your outlines and try out different color schemes from this assortment to see which ones enhance your design the most.

- **For those who love crafting and DIY projects**, each page of the palette includes the Hex, RGB and CYMK color codes for all six colors used. This simplifies the process of incorporating these colors into your creative projects.

Anatomy of a palette page

On each palette page you will find the following information:
1. The image inspiration
2. Hex, RGB and CYMK Color codes for various craft projects like coloring or scrapbooking
3. DMC 6 strand floss thread code and image

How to Use the Palettes

Each palette is inspired by a particular season, making it easy to choose colors that complement each other perfectly. To use a palette, simply select one of the colors from the list and start stitching! You can use as many or as few of the colors as you like, depending on your project.

One helpful tip when using the palettes is to consider light and dark values. Mixing light and dark shades within a single palette can create depth and interest in your finished project. Another technique is to use complementary colors next to each other for added vibrancy. It's also important to keep in mind that different lighting situations may affect how certain colors appear, so be sure to test out your chosen color combinations in various lighting conditions before committing.

Overall, using these color palettes can help take your cross-stitching projects to the next level. With their expertly curated combinations inspired by seasons, they make selecting thread flosses an easier task for stitchers.

The warmth of apple-picking

Hex, RGB and CMYK Color Details

	HEX	RGB	CMYK
	#442F1F	68,47,31	0,31,54,73
	#7A6B3B	122,107,59	0,12,52,52
	#e88551	232,133,81	0,43,65,9
	#C7AC58	199,172,88	0,14,56,22
	#97907D	151,144,125	0,5,17,41
	#D9D5A0	217,213,160	0,2,26,15

Embroidery Thread Conversion Chart

	DMC	Name
	DMC 839	Dark Beige Brown
	DMC 3012	Medium Khaki Green
	DMC 722	Light Orange Spice
	DMC 734	Light Olive Green
	DMC 3023	Light Brown Gray
	DMC 772	Very Light Yellow Green

Mushrooms in vibrant shades of red popping through freshly fallen leaves

Hex, RGB and CMYK Color Details

	HEX	RGB	CMYK
	#211E0C	33,30,12	0,9,64,87
	#373D0F	55,61,15	10,0,75,76
	#8C0303	140,3,3	0,98,98,45
	#3E5902	62,89,2	30,0,98,65
	#A5180F	165,24,15	0,85,91,35
	#594D3D	89,77,61	0,13,31,65

Embroidery Thread Conversion Chart

	DMC 934 Black Avocado Green
	DMC 3345 Dark Hunter Green
	DMC 817 Very Dark Coral Red
	DMC 905 Dark Parrot Green
	DMC 606 Bright Orange-Red
	DMC 3787 Dark Brown Gray

A splash of blue in an autumn landscape

Hex, RGB and CMYK Color Details

	HEX	RGB	CMYK
	#402401	64,36,1	0,44,98,75
	#2D2C19	45,44,25	0,2,44,82
	#1F4C73	31,76,115	73,34,0,55
	#575912	87,89,18	2,0,80,65
	#735826	115,88,38	0,23,67,55
	#A9B6A7	169,182,167	7,0,8,29

Embroidery Thread Conversion Chart

	DMC 898 Very Dark Coffee Brown
	DMC 934 Black Avocado Green
	DMC 312 Very Dark Baby Blue
	DMC 469 Avocado Green
	DMC 869 Very Dark Hazelnut Brown
	DMC 3817 Light Celadon Green

A breathtaking view of the church as autumn falls around it

Hex, RGB and CMYK Color Details

	HEX	RGB	CMYK
	#212121	33,33,33	0,0,0,87
	#4D5057	77,80,87	11,8,0,66
	#A64F03	166,79,3	0,52,98,35
	#AA7620	170,118,32	0,31,81,33
	#D9A404	217,164,4	0,24,98,15
	#9CD9D3	156,217,211	28,0,3,15

Embroidery Thread Conversion Chart

	DMC 3799 Very Dark Pewter Gray
	DMC 317 Pewter Gray
	DMC 720 Dark Orange Spice
	DMC 832 Golden Olive
	DMC 728 Topaz
	DMC 964 Light Seagreen

Feel the crisp fall air against the majestic mountain backdrop

Hex, RGB and CMYK Color Details

	HEX	RGB	CMYK
	#23130C	35,19,12	0,46,66,86
	#594302	89,67,2	0,25,98,65
	#553D35	85,61,53	0,28,38,67
	#A15C35	161,92,53	0,43,67,37
	#697694	105,118,148	29,20,0,42
	#A4ABB9	164,171,185	11,8,0,27

Embroidery Thread Conversion Chart

	DMC 3371 — Black Brown
	DMC 730 — Very Dark Olive Green
	DMC 779 — Dark Cocoa
	DMC 435 — Very Light Brown
	DMC 793 — Medium Cornflower Blue
	DMC 159 — Light Gray Blue

Autumn mornings are best spent curled up with a cup of coffee and an inspiring book.

Hex, RGB and CMYK Color Details

	HEX	RGB	CMYK
	#2C231B	44,35,27	0,20,39,83
	#8C2626	140,38,38	0,73,73,45
	#594438	89,68,56	0,24,37,65
	#BF6849	191,104,73	0,46,62,25
	#F2C094	242,192,148	0,21,39,5
	#F2E0DC	242,224,220	0,7,9,5

Embroidery Thread Conversion Chart

	DMC 3021 — Very Dark Brown Gray
	DMC 347 — Very Dark Salmon
	DMC 08 — Dark Driftwood
	DMC 922 — Light Copper
	DMC 3856 — Ultra Very Light Mahogany
	DMC 819 — Light Baby Pink

Seasonal hues of colors spread around us in magical ways

Hex, RGB and CMYK Color Details

	HEX	RGB	CMYK
	#1D3331	29,51,49	43,0,4,80
	#8C0327	140,3,39	0,98,72,45
	#0C68AD	12,104,173	93,40,0,32
	#8C7503	140,117,3	0,16,98,45
	#C7962F	199,150,47	0,25,76,22
	#16B9F9	22,185,249	91,26,0,2

Embroidery Thread Conversion Chart

	DMC 924 Very Dark Gray Green
	DMC 347 Very Dark Salmon
	DMC 798 Dark Delft Blue
	DMC 733 Medium Olive Green
	DMC 3820 Dark Straw
	DMC 996 Medium Electric Blue

A truly mesmerizing display of all the colors of autumn

Hex, RGB and CMYK Color Details

	HEX	RGB	CMYK
	#442213	68,34,19	0,50,72,73
	#864332	134,67,50	0,50,63,47
	#EB535E	235,83,94	0,65,60,8
	#DF9C27	223,156,39	0,30,83,13
	#E683CD	230,131,205	0,43,11,10
	#D19D51	209,157,81	0,25,61,18

Embroidery Thread Conversion Chart

DMC 898	Very Dark Coffee Brown
DMC 356	Medium Terra Cotta
DMC 3801	Very Dark Melon
DMC 728	Topaz
DMC 3607	Light Plum
DMC 834	Very Light Golden Olive

The perfect winter evening pick-me-up

Hex, RGB and CMYK Color Details

	HEX	RGB	CMYK
	HEX #244026	RGB 36,64,38	CMYK 44,0,41,75
	HEX #684A33	RGB 104,74,51	CMYK 0,29,51,59
	HEX #8D6B50	RGB 141,107,80	CMYK 0,24,43,45
	HEX #B29381	RGB 178,147,129	CMYK 0,17,28,30
	HEX #C9B1A7	RGB 201,177,167	CMYK 0,12,17,21
	HEX #D4D8DE	RGB 212,216,222	CMYK 5,3,0,13

Embroidery Thread Conversion Chart

	DMC 319 Very Dark Pistachio Green
	DMC 3862 Dark Mocha Beige
	DMC 3863 Medium Mocha Beige
	DMC 841 Light Beige Brown
	DMC 06 Medium Light Driftwood
	DMC 3753 Ultra Very Light Antique Blue

Looks like this witch is ready

Hex, RGB and CMYK Color Details

	HEX	RGB	CMYK
	#271C2A	39,28,42	7,33,0,84
	#8C4646	140,70,70	0,50,50,45
	#7C5650	124,86,80	0,31,35,51
	#D97855	217,120,85	0,45,61,15
	#BF8E76	191,142,118	0,26,38,25
	#BFADA8	191,173,168	0,9,12,25

Embroidery Thread Conversion Chart

	DMC 29 Eggplant
	DMC 3721 Dark Shell Pink
	DMC 3860 Cocoa
	DMC 3340 Medium Apricot
	DMC 758 Very Light Terra Cotta
	DMC 06 Medium Light Driftwood

Fall is here, and so are the seasonal vegetables

Hex, RGB and CMYK Color Details

	HEX	RGB	CMYK
	#172601	23,38,1	39,0,97,85
	#732002	115,32,2	0,72,98,55
	#5F3F27	95,63,39	0,34,59,63
	#D4410E	212,65,14	0,69,93,17
	#8F6D4A	143,109,74	0,24,48,44
	#F4910E	244,145,14	0,41,94,4

Embroidery Thread Conversion Chart

	DMC 890 Ultra Dark Pistachio Green
	DMC 919 Red Copper
	DMC 3862 Dark Mocha Beige
	DMC 608 Bright Orange
	DMC 3863 Medium Mocha Beige
	DMC 741 Medium Tangerine

A fall morning of cozy reading

Hex, RGB and CMYK Color Details

	HEX	RGB	CMYK
	#594B37	89,75,55	0,16,38,65
	#735F4D	115,95,77	0,17,33,55
	#657334	101,115,52	12,0,55,55
	#F29F05	242,159,5	0,34,98,5
	#B89E67	184,158,103	0,14,44,28
	#E9DABB	233,218,187	0,6,20,9

Embroidery Thread Conversion Chart

	DMC 3787 Dark Brown Gray
	DMC 3790 Ultra Dark Beige Gray
	DMC 988 Medium Forest Green
	DMC 972 Deep Canary
	DMC 422 Light Hazelnut Brown
	DMC 739 Ultra Very Light Tan

Juicy and bright red berries

Hex, RGB and CMYK Color Details

	HEX	RGB	CMYK
	#6F0C08	111,12,8	0,89,93,56
	#A60303	166,3,3	0,98,98,35
	#59554C	89,85,76	0,4,15,65
	#9F816C	159,129,108	0,19,32,38
	#C88971	200,137,113	0,32,44,22
	#E0B59F	224,181,159	0,19,29,12

Embroidery Thread Conversion Chart

	DMC 919 Red Copper
	DMC 606 Bright Orange-Red
	DMC 645 Very Dark Beaver Gray
	DMC 841 Light Beige Brown
	DMC 352 Light Coral
	DMC 754 Light Peach

A stunning road of literally autumn art

Hex, RGB and CMYK Color Details

	HEX	RGB	CMYK
	#400101	64,1,1	0,98,98,75
	#A60321	166,3,33	0,98,80,35
	#48454B	72,69,75	4,8,0,71
	#943136	148,49,54	0,67,64,42
	#5E666B	94,102,107	12,5,0,58
	#D7D9D9	215,217,217	1,0,0,15

Embroidery Thread Conversion Chart

	DMC 814 Dark Garnet
	DMC 666 Bright Red
	DMC 535 Very Light Ash Gray
	DMC 309 Dark Rose
	DMC 414 Dark Steel Gray
	DMC 762 Very Light Pearl Gray

Sun-kissed trees in a peaceful forest

Hex, RGB and CMYK Color Details

	HEX	RGB	CMYK
	#590202	89,2,2	0,98,98,65
	#595302	89,83,2	0,7,98,65
	#8B4B1F	139,75,31	0,46,78,45
	#AC7736	172,119,54	0,31,69,33
	#AA9347	170,147,71	0,14,58,33
	#EEE2C4	238,226,196	0,5,18,7

Embroidery Thread Conversion Chart

	DMC 3777 Very Dark Terra Cotta
	DMC 580 Dark Moss Green
	DMC 301 Medium Mahogany
	DMC 680 Dark Old Gold
	DMC 734 Light Olive Green
	DMC 746 Off White

Warm up with a cozy cup of tea and soak in the beautiful autumn scenery

Hex, RGB and CMYK Color Details

	HEX	RGB	CMYK
	#6C5220	108,82,32	0,24,70,58
	#A64F03	166,79,3	0,52,98,35
	#8C7C68	140,124,104	0,11,26,45
	#F2B705	242,183,5	0,24,98,5
	#BFB741	191,183,65	0,4,66,25
	#D9D1A9	217,209,169	0,4,22,15

Embroidery Thread Conversion Chart

	DMC 869 Very Dark Hazelnut Brown
	DMC 720 Dark Orange Spice
	DMC 07 Driftwood
	DMC 444 Dark Lemon
	DMC 12 Tender Green
	DMC 772 Very Light Yellow Green

Fiery red leaves twirling in the autumn breeze

Hex, RGB and CMYK Color Details

	HEX	RGB	CMYK
	#8A1925	138,25,37	0,82,73,46
	#AB3F55	171,63,85	0,63,50,33
	#647F3D	100,127,61	21,0,52,50
	#C96B87	201,107,135	0,47,33,21
	#8EA060	142,160,96	11,0,40,37
	#C1B7AA	193,183,170	0,5,12,24

Embroidery Thread Conversion Chart

	DMC 347 Very Dark Salmon
	DMC 3832 Medium Raspberry
	DMC 988 Medium Forest Green
	DMC 961 Dark Dusty Rose
	DMC 989 Forest Green
	DMC 05 Light Driftwood

17

Golden leaves, crisp air, and a mystical broomstick

Hex, RGB and CMYK Color Details

	HEX	RGB	CMYK
	#170C03	23,12,3	0,48,87,91
	#4C290B	76,41,11	0,46,86,70
	#8A5922	138,89,34	0,36,75,46
	#B18A5A	177,138,90	0,22,49,31
	#EFAF32	239,175,50	0,27,79,6
	#ECCA82	236,202,130	0,14,45,7

Embroidery Thread Conversion Chart

	DMC 3371 — Black Brown
	DMC 801 — Dark Coffee Brown
	DMC 420 — Dark Hazelnut Brown
	DMC 3045 — Dark Yellow Beige
	DMC 725 — Medium Light Topaz
	DMC 744 — Pale Yellow

The vibrant cozy colors of Girona at peak autumn season

Hex, RGB and CMYK Color Details

	HEX	RGB	CMYK
	#4E4433	78,68,51	0,13,35,69
	#D9805F	217,128,95	0,41,56,15
	#D9A23D	217,162,61	0,25,72,15
	#77A1D9	119,161,217	45,26,0,15
	#B39D7C	179,157,124	0,12,31,30
	#CED6E5	206,214,229	10,7,0,10

Embroidery Thread Conversion Chart

	DMC 3787 Dark Brown Gray
	DMC 3341 Apricot
	DMC 3820 Dark Straw
	DMC 3839 Medium Lavender Blue
	DMC 612 Light Drab Brown
	DMC 3747 Very Light Blue Violet

An aura of warmth and cozy spirit

Hex, RGB and CMYK Color Details

	HEX	RGB	CMYK
	#76120C	118,18,12	0,85,90,54
	#BD1A16	189,26,22	0,86,88,26
	#629525	98,149,37	34,0,75,42
	#C36E56	195,110,86	0,44,56,24
	#0997A0	9,151,160	94,6,0,37
	#D1B79C	209,183,156	0,12,25,18

Embroidery Thread Conversion Chart

	DMC 919 Red Copper
	DMC 606 Bright Orange-Red
	DMC 906 Medium Parrot Green
	DMC 21 Light Alizarin
	DMC 3845 Medium Bright Turquoise
	DMC 950 Light Desert Sand

Finding balance in the chaos of everyday life

Hex, RGB and CMYK Color Details

	HEX	RGB	CMYK
	#34332E	52,51,46	0,2,12,80
	#065B52	6,91,82	93,0,10,64
	#B74E07	183,78,7	0,57,96,28
	#038C73	3,140,115	98,0,18,45
	#DC883D	220,136,61	0,38,72,14
	#F1DCCD	241,220,205	0,9,15,5

Embroidery Thread Conversion Chart

	DMC 3799 Very Dark Pewter Gray
	DMC 3847 Dark Teal Green
	DMC 720 Dark Orange Spice
	DMC 3812 Very Dark Seagreen
	DMC 3853 Dark Autumn Gold
	DMC 3770 Very Light Tawny

Captivating sun rays dancing through the autumn leaves

Hex, RGB and CMYK Color Details

	HEX	RGB	CMYK
	#0D0D0D	13,13,13	0,0,0,95
	#153A67	21,58,103	80,44,0,60
	#A61F38	166,31,56	0,81,66,35
	#585C66	88,92,102	14,10,0,60
	#AB8D8B	171,141,139	0,18,19,33
	#F2EB88	242,235,136	0,3,44,5

Embroidery Thread Conversion Chart

	DMC 310 — Black
	DMC 824 — Very Dark Blue
	DMC 3801 — Very Dark Melon
	DMC 317 — Pewter Gray
	DMC 3861 — Light Cocoa
	DMC 445 — Light Lemon

The colorful trees reflecting off the glassy lake

Hex, RGB and CMYK Color Details

	HEX	RGB	CMYK
	#3B2B19	59,43,25	0,27,58,77
	#38442C	56,68,44	18,0,35,73
	#44603A	68,96,58	29,0,40,62
	#695B35	105,91,53	0,13,50,59
	#D96704	217,103,4	0,53,98,15
	#D9A404	217,164,4	0,24,98,15

Embroidery Thread Conversion Chart

	DMC 3031 — Very Dark Mocha Brown
	DMC 520 — Dark Fern Green
	DMC 367 — Dark Pistachio Green
	DMC 3011 — Dark Khaki Green
	DMC 740 — Tangerine
	DMC 728 — Topaz

A full fall glory

Hex, RGB and CMYK Color Details

	HEX	RGB	CMYK
	#3E2D15	62,45,21	0,27,66,76
	#A65D03	166,93,3	0,44,98,35
	#A0A603	160,166,3	4,0,98,35
	#C6AE99	198,174,153	0,12,23,22
	#ACD7F2	172,215,242	29,11,0,5
	#E8DCDE	232,220,222	0,5,4,9

Embroidery Thread Conversion Chart

	DMC 3781 Dark Mocha Brown
	DMC 782 Dark Topaz
	DMC 907 Light Parrot Green
	DMC 842 Very Light Beige Brown
	DMC 3840 Light Lavender Blue
	DMC 24 White Lavender

It's the perfect fall day for a picnic

Hex, RGB and CMYK Color Details

	HEX	RGB	CMYK
	HEX #615535	RGB 97,85,53	CMYK 0,12,45,62
	HEX #D93B18	RGB 217,59,24	CMYK 0,73,89,15
	HEX #C9623A	RGB 201,98,58	CMYK 0,51,71,21
	HEX #8E805B	RGB 142,128,91	CMYK 0,10,36,44
	HEX #BDCAF2	RGB 189,202,242	CMYK 22,17,0,5
	HEX #F2EFC4	RGB 242,239,196	CMYK 0,1,19,5

Embroidery Thread Conversion Chart

	DMC 3011 Dark Khaki Green
	DMC 608 Bright Orange
	DMC 922 Light Copper
	DMC 3052 Medium Green Gray
	DMC 26 Pale Lavender
	DMC 3823 Ultra Pale Yellow

The beauty of a winter wonderland

Hex, RGB and CMYK Color Details

	HEX	RGB	CMYK
	#2E1E21	46,30,33	0,35,28,82
	#89706F	137,112,111	0,18,19,46
	#608CAB	96,140,171	44,18,0,33
	#0373BF	3,115,191	98,40,0,25
	#23456E	35,69,110	68,37,0,57
	#D1B8A4	209,184,164	0,12,22,18

Embroidery Thread Conversion Chart

	DMC 09 Very Dark Cocoa
	DMC 451 Dark Shell Gray
	DMC 334 Medium Baby Blue
	DMC 798 Dark Delft Blue
	DMC 158 Very Dark Cornflower Blue
	DMC 950 Light Desert Sand

The sky paints a beautiful winter masterpiece

Hex, RGB and CMYK Color Details

	HEX	RGB	CMYK
	#081723	8,23,35	77,34,0,86
	#132D55	19,45,85	78,47,0,67
	#435C73	67,92,115	42,20,0,55
	#948BB8	148,139,184	20,24,0,28
	#B2A0D9	178,160,217	18,26,0,15
	#D6BAD3	214,186,211	0,13,1,16

Embroidery Thread Conversion Chart

	DMC 939 Very Dark Navy Blue
	DMC 158 Very Dark Cornflower Blue
	DMC 161 Gray Blue
	DMC 209 Dark Lavender
	DMC 210 Medium Lavender
	DMC 153 Very Light Violet

Festive times and sparkling lights

Hex, RGB and CMYK Color Details

	HEX	RGB	CMYK
	#590202	89,2,2	0,98,98,65
	#274001	39,64,1	39,0,98,75
	#8C0F0F	140,15,15	0,89,89,45
	#8D6F4A	141,111,74	0,21,48,45
	#BF7E45	191,126,69	0,34,64,25
	#D9B9A7	217,185,167	0,15,23,15

Embroidery Thread Conversion Chart

	DMC 3777 Very Dark Terra Cotta
	DMC 986 Very Dark Forest Green
	DMC 817 Very Dark Coral Red
	DMC 3863 Medium Mocha Beige
	DMC 977 Light Golden Brown
	DMC 950 Light Desert Sand

Ready to spread some holiday cheer

Hex, RGB and CMYK Color Details

	HEX	RGB	CMYK
	#283E6D	40,62,109	63,43,0,57
	#4A3E2B	74,62,43	0,16,42,71
	#9A1613	154,22,19	0,86,88,40
	#285FB8	40,95,184	78,48,0,28
	#97785F	151,120,95	0,21,37,41
	#CCB395	204,179,149	0,12,27,20

Embroidery Thread Conversion Chart

	DMC 158 — Very Dark Cornflower Blue
	DMC 839 — Dark Beige Brown
	DMC 666 — Bright Red
	DMC 3746 — Dark Blue Violet
	DMC 3863 — Medium Mocha Beige
	DMC 738 — Very Light Tan

Cute christmas dolls sparkled in snow

Hex, RGB and CMYK Color Details

	HEX	RGB	CMYK
	#362020	54,32,32	0,41,41,79
	#A12331	161,35,49	0,78,70,37
	#5B6263	91,98,99	8,1,0,61
	#8B8F8D	139,143,141	3,0,1,44
	#B3B7B3	179,183,179	2,0,2,28
	#DAE3E4	218,227,228	4,0,0,11

Embroidery Thread Conversion Chart

	DMC 838 Very Dark Beige Brown
	DMC 347 Very Dark Salmon
	DMC 3768 Dark Gray Green
	DMC 169 Light Pewter
	DMC 168 Very Light Pewter
	DMC 27 White Violet

The silent night of the forest, illuminated only by softly-falling snowflakes

Hex, RGB and CMYK Color Details

HEX	RGB	CMYK
#101C33	16,28,51	69,45,0,80
#1B2E56	27,46,86	69,47,0,66
#284177	40,65,119	66,45,0,53
#395C9D	57,92,157	64,41,0,38
#5582CD	85,130,205	59,37,0,20
#85B7F6	133,183,246	46,26,0,4

Embroidery Thread Conversion Chart

DMC 823	Dark Navy Blue
DMC 158	Very Dark Cornflower Blue
DMC 797	Royal Blue
DMC 3746	Dark Blue Violet
DMC 340	Medium Blue Violet
DMC 341	Light Blue Violet

No matter how cold the winter may be, this beautiful bird's spirit is warmer than ever

Hex, RGB and CMYK Color Details

	HEX	RGB	CMYK
	#30251D	48,37,29	0,23,40,81
	#675C57	103,92,87	0,11,16,60
	#7A7271	122,114,113	0,7,7,52
	#90888B	144,136,139	0,6,3,44
	#9A9EB6	154,158,182	15,13,0,29
	#E4D9D4	228,217,212	0,5,7,11

Embroidery Thread Conversion Chart

	DMC 3021	Very Dark Brown Gray
	DMC 645	Very Dark Beaver Gray
	DMC 04	Dark Tin
	DMC 415	Pearl Gray
	DMC 159	Light Gray Blue
	DMC 3866	Ultra Very Light Mocha

Magical winter wonderland

Hex, RGB and CMYK Color Details

	HEX	RGB	CMYK
	#232426	35,36,38	8,5,0,85
	#59221D	89,34,29	0,62,67,65
	#834F3F	131,79,63	0,40,52,49
	#4C626D	76,98,109	30,10,0,57
	#7B8A8F	123,138,143	14,3,0,44
	#BCCECA	188,206,202	9,0,2,19

Embroidery Thread Conversion Chart

	DMC 3799 Very Dark Pewter Gray
	DMC 221 Very Dark Shell Pink
	DMC 3772 Very Dark Desert Sand
	DMC 3768 Dark Gray Green
	DMC 926 Medium Gray Green
	DMC 3811 Very Light Turquoise

The snowflakes fall softly and the lantern glows brightly

Hex, RGB and CMYK Color Details

	HEX	RGB	CMYK
	#12131C	18,19,28	36,32,0,89
	#575C73	87,92,115	24,20,0,55
	#F2EB80	242,235,128	0,3,47,5
	#F2B05E	242,176,94	0,27,61,5
	#BAC2D9	186,194,217	14,11,0,15
	#C6BEBE	198,190,190	0,4,4,22

Embroidery Thread Conversion Chart

	DMC 939 Very Dark Navy Blue
	DMC 161 Gray Blue
	DMC 445 Light Lemon
	DMC 725 Medium Light Topaz
	DMC 26 Pale Lavender
	DMC 02 Tin

Majestic winter snow owl

Hex, RGB and CMYK Color Details

	HEX	RGB	CMYK
	#243644	36,54,68	47,21,0,73
	#748CAA	116,140,170	32,18,0,33
	#FFEF03	255,239,3	0,6,99,0
	#7EA5D9	126,165,217	42,24,0,15
	#B9D5EA	185,213,234	21,9,0,8
	#C2E5F2	194,229,242	20,5,0,5

Embroidery Thread Conversion Chart

	DMC	
	DMC 3750	Very Dark Antique Blue
	DMC 160	Medium Gray Blue
	DMC 307	Lemon
	DMC 3839	Medium Lavender Blue
	DMC 800	Pale Delft Blue
	DMC 747	Very Light Sky Blue

The snow may be cold, but this bright red sparrow warms our hearts

Hex, RGB and CMYK Color Details

	HEX	RGB	CMYK
	#B41117	180,17,23	0,91,87,29
	#525A67	82,90,103	20,13,0,60
	#8A7F7C	138,127,124	0,8,10,46
	#868488	134,132,136	1,3,0,47
	#91AEC9	145,174,201	28,13,0,21
	#E2EBF5	226,235,245	8,4,0,4

Embroidery Thread Conversion Chart

	DMC 606 — Bright Orange-Red
	DMC 317 — Pewter Gray
	DMC 07 — Driftwood
	DMC 169 — Light Pewter
	DMC 341 — Light Blue Violet
	DMC 3756 — Ultra Very Light Baby Blue

This magical time of year calls for a slice (or two) of a heavenly Christmas chocolate cake

Hex, RGB and CMYK Color Details

	HEX	RGB	CMYK
	#354F20	53,79,32	33,0,59,69
	#694036	105,64,54	0,39,49,59
	#BB331E	187,51,30	0,73,84,27
	#D28141	210,129,65	0,39,69,18
	#D3A838	211,168,56	0,20,73,17
	#CBCBCC	203,203,204	0,0,0,20

Embroidery Thread Conversion Chart

	DMC 986 Very Dark Forest Green
	DMC 632 Ultra Very Dark Desert Sand
	DMC 606 Bright Orange-Red
	DMC 976 Medium Golden Brown
	DMC 3821 Straw
	DMC 01 White Tin

These cozy blue gloves can handle even the biggest snowflakes

Hex, RGB and CMYK Color Details

	HEX	RGB	CMYK
	#45596E	69,89,110	37,19,0,57
	#688499	104,132,153	32,14,0,40
	#86A1B5	134,161,181	26,11,0,29
	#9EB9CD	158,185,205	23,10,0,20
	#B5CDDF	181,205,223	19,8,0,13
	#D9E2EA	217,226,234	7,3,0,8

Embroidery Thread Conversion Chart

	DMC 161 Gray Blue
	DMC 931 Medium Antique Blue
	DMC 932 Light Antique Blue
	DMC 157 Very Light Cornflower Blue
	DMC 800 Pale Delft Blue
	DMC 27 White Violet

Happy snowman

Hex, RGB and CMYK Color Details

	HEX	RGB	CMYK
	#1F1A1F	31,26,31	0,16,0,88
	#5A5B71	90,91,113	20,19,0,56
	#E34848	227,72,72	0,68,68,11
	#6C836C	108,131,108	18,0,18,49
	#9E9FA6	158,159,166	5,4,0,35
	#FCF4EA	252,244,234	0,3,7,1

Embroidery Thread Conversion Chart

	DMC 939 Very Dark Navy Blue
	DMC 161 Gray Blue
	DMC 3801 Very Dark Melon
	DMC 502 Blue Green
	DMC 318 Light Steel Gray
	DMC 3865 Winter White

The perfect winter-scape

Hex, RGB and CMYK Color Details

	HEX	RGB	CMYK
	#01402E	1,64,46	98,0,28,75
	#8C6354	140,99,84	0,29,40,45
	#656867	101,104,103	3,0,1,59
	#49868C	73,134,140	48,4,0,45
	#D9BDAD	217,189,173	0,13,20,15
	#D9DDDB	217,221,219	2,0,1,13

Embroidery Thread Conversion Chart

	DMC 3847 — Dark Teal Green
	DMC 3772 — Very Dark Desert Sand
	DMC 04 — Dark Tin
	DMC 3810 — Dark Turquoise
	DMC 950 — Light Desert Sand
	DMC 762 — Very Light Pearl Gray

All aboard for an incredible winter adventure!

Hex, RGB and CMYK Color Details

	HEX	RGB	CMYK
	#261E20	38,30,32	0,21,16,85
	#590A18	89,10,24	0,89,73,65
	#404040	64,64,64	0,0,0,75
	#8C2218	140,34,24	0,76,83,45
	#A8A9AC	168,169,172	2,2,0,33
	#C7CDD2	199,205,210	5,2,0,18

Embroidery Thread Conversion Chart

	DMC 3799 Very Dark Pewter Gray
	DMC 221 Very Dark Shell Pink
	DMC 535 Very Light Ash Gray
	DMC 817 Very Dark Coral Red
	DMC 03 Medium Tin
	DMC 3753 Ultra Very Light Antique Blue

Nothing like a warm cup of coffee to make winter's chill go away

Hex, RGB and CMYK Color Details

	HEX	RGB	CMYK
	#942839	148,40,57	0,73,61,42
	#B98974	185,137,116	0,26,37,27
	#CAACA6	202,172,166	0,15,18,21
	#D4C9D1	212,201,209	0,5,1,17
	#EAE8EE	234,232,238	2,3,0,7
	#F0F0F2	240,240,242	1,1,0,5

Embroidery Thread Conversion Chart

	DMC 3831 — Dark Raspberry
	DMC 407 — Dark Desert Sand
	DMC 224 — Very Light Shell Pink
	DMC 3743 — Very Light Antique Violet
	DMC 27 — White Violet
	DMC B5200 — Snow White

The snow-covered trees twinkle in the sun, creating a mesmerizing view.

Hex, RGB and CMYK Color Details

	HEX	RGB	CMYK
	#080D06	8,13,6	38,0,54,95
	#2E2F1E	46,47,30	2,0,36,82
	#5B4F35	91,79,53	0,13,42,64
	#81755D	129,117,93	0,9,28,49
	#CC9F57	204,159,87	0,22,57,20
	#B4B4AA	180,180,170	0,0,6,29

Embroidery Thread Conversion Chart

	DMC 310 — Black
	DMC 934 — Black Avocado Green
	DMC 3787 — Dark Brown Gray
	DMC 640 — Very Dark Beige Gray
	DMC 834 — Very Light Golden Olive
	DMC 06 — Medium Light Driftwood

Take a deep breath and marvel at the beauty of this stunning winter sunset

Hex, RGB and CMYK Color Details

	HEX	RGB	CMYK
	#50295A	80,41,90	11,54,0,65
	#7E4B95	126,75,149	15,50,0,42
	#B85870	184,88,112	0,52,39,28
	#B76CAF	183,108,175	0,41,4,28
	#F76F5F	247,111,95	0,55,62,3
	#FEA088	254,160,136	0,37,46,0

Embroidery Thread Conversion Chart

	DMC 3834 — Dark Grape
	DMC 208 — Very Dark Lavender
	DMC 335 — Rose
	DMC 3607 — Light Plum
	DMC 3340 — Medium Apricot
	DMC 3341 — Apricot

Nature's beauty is truly breathtaking

Hex, RGB and CMYK Color Details

	HEX	RGB	CMYK
	#403436	64,52,54	0,19,16,75
	#6F87A6	111,135,166	33,19,0,35
	#82818D	130,129,141	8,9,0,45
	#F2994B	242,153,75	0,37,69,5
	#F2EB80	242,235,128	0,3,47,5
	#EAB88A	234,184,138	0,21,41,8

Embroidery Thread Conversion Chart

	DMC 09 — Very Dark Cocoa
	DMC 160 — Medium Gray Blue
	DMC 414 — Dark Steel Gray
	DMC 3854 — Medium Autumn Gold
	DMC 445 — Light Lemon
	DMC 3856 — Ultra Very Light Mahogany

Fascinating ice sculpture lit up by sparkling snow

Hex, RGB and CMYK Color Details

	HEX	RGB	CMYK
	#4A617D	74,97,125	41,22,0,51
	#6E8094	110,128,148	26,14,0,42
	#7AB3BF	122,179,191	36,6,0,25
	#B9C1CB	185,193,203	9,5,0,20
	#E2E6EB	226,230,235	4,2,0,8
	#F2F2F2	242,242,242	0,0,0,5

Embroidery Thread Conversion Chart

	DMC 161 — Gray Blue
	DMC 160 — Medium Gray Blue
	DMC 519 — Sky Blue
	DMC 3752 — Very Light Antique Blue
	DMC 27 — White Violet
	DMC B5200 — Snow White

This magical festive scene has it all

Hex, RGB and CMYK Color Details

	HEX	RGB	CMYK
	HEX #73020C	RGB 115,2,12	CMYK 0,98,90,55
	HEX #A60321	RGB 166,3,33	CMYK 0,98,80,35
	HEX #735236	RGB 115,82,54	CMYK 0,29,53,55
	HEX #8E6D6B	RGB 142,109,107	CMYK 0,23,25,44
	HEX #AD979A	RGB 173,151,154	CMYK 0,13,11,32
	HEX #BFAEA8	RGB 191,174,168	CMYK 0,9,12,25

Embroidery Thread Conversion Chart

	DMC 321 Red
	DMC 666 Bright Red
	DMC 3862 Dark Mocha Beige
	DMC 451 Dark Shell Gray
	DMC 3042 Light Antique Violet
	DMC 06 Medium Light Driftwood

Toronto is a beautiful city all year round, and winter doesn't take away from it

Hex, RGB and CMYK Color Details

	HEX	RGB	CMYK
	#BF2604	191,38,4	0,80,98,25
	#4D6671	77,102,113	32,10,0,56
	#BF9004	191,144,4	0,25,98,25
	#65818C	101,129,140	28,8,0,45
	#52ABA9	82,171,169	52,0,1,33
	#96A3AA	150,163,170	12,4,0,33

Embroidery Thread Conversion Chart

	DMC 608 Bright Orange	
	DMC 3768 Dark Gray Green	
	DMC 3820 Dark Straw	
	DMC 931 Medium Antique Blue	
	DMC 958 Dark Seagreen	
	DMC 318 Light Steel Gray	

The enchanting hues of a winter sunset

Hex, RGB and CMYK Color Details

	HEX	RGB	CMYK
	#281A5C	40,26,92	57,72,0,64
	#611A52	97,26,82	0,73,15,62
	#673698	103,54,152	32,64,0,40
	#B13C7C	177,60,124	0,66,30,31
	#C5456C	197,69,108	0,65,45,23
	#DF5970	223,89,112	0,60,50,13

Embroidery Thread Conversion Chart

	DMC 820 Very Dark Royal Blue
	DMC 34 Dark Fuchsia
	DMC 3837 Ultra Dark Lavender
	DMC 3804 Dark Cyclamen Pink
	DMC 335 Rose
	DMC 892 Medium Carnation

Ginger and lemon add the perfect amount of zing to snowy days

Hex, RGB and CMYK Color Details

	HEX	RGB	CMYK
	#2A1D11	42,29,17	0,31,60,84
	#534539	83,69,57	0,17,31,67
	#BF3604	191,54,4	0,72,98,25
	#BF6B04	191,107,4	0,44,98,25
	#B0821C	176,130,28	0,26,84,31
	#D9AF32	217,175,50	0,19,77,15

Embroidery Thread Conversion Chart

	DMC 3021 Very Dark Brown Gray
	DMC 08 Dark Driftwood
	DMC 608 Bright Orange
	DMC 3853 Dark Autumn Gold
	DMC 833 Light Golden Olive
	DMC 18 Yellow Plum

A picture-perfect bouquet of blue hydrangeas

Hex, RGB and CMYK Color Details

	HEX	RGB	CMYK
	HEX #2C2525	RGB 44,37,37	CMYK 0,16,16,83
	HEX #314159	RGB 49,65,89	CMYK 45,27,0,65
	HEX #0E4E97	RGB 14,78,151	CMYK 91,48,0,41
	HEX #688BB6	RGB 104,139,182	CMYK 43,24,0,29
	HEX #8EAED4	RGB 142,174,212	CMYK 33,18,0,17
	HEX #B9D0E8	RGB 185,208,232	CMYK 20,10,0,9

Embroidery Thread Conversion Chart

	DMC 3799 Very Dark Pewter Gray
	DMC 312 Very Dark Baby Blue
	DMC 792 Dark Cornflower Blue
	DMC 3839 Medium Lavender Blue
	DMC 809 Delft Blue
	DMC 3840 Light Lavender Blue

Spring is in full bloom

Hex, RGB and CMYK Color Details

	HEX	RGB	CMYK
	#0F1C20	15,28,32	53,13,0,87
	#054563	5,69,99	95,30,0,61
	#208278	32,130,120	75,0,8,49
	#6F8666	111,134,102	17,0,24,47
	#69B8AD	105,184,173	43,0,6,28
	#C8D5D3	200,213,211	6,0,1,16

Embroidery Thread Conversion Chart

	DMC 310 — Black
	DMC 3842 — Very Dark Wedgwood
	DMC 3848 — Medium Teal Green
	DMC 320 — Medium Pistachio Green
	DMC 959 — Medium Seagreen
	DMC 775 — Very Light Baby Blue

A gorgeous butterfly flitting its way through a field of vibrant wildflowers

Hex, RGB and CMYK Color Details

	HEX	RGB	CMYK
	#2D5127	45,81,39	44,0,52,68
	#477D45	71,125,69	43,0,45,51
	#E8950F	232,149,15	0,36,94,9
	#7A9975	122,153,117	20,0,24,40
	#93B8CB	147,184,203	28,9,0,20
	#ECD1B1	236,209,177	0,11,25,7

Embroidery Thread Conversion Chart

	DMC 986 Very Dark Forest Green
	DMC 912 Light Emerald Green
	DMC 972 Deep Canary
	DMC 3816 Celadon Green
	DMC 519 Sky Blue
	DMC 739 Ultra Very Light Tan

Picturesque petals of blooming flowers, dancing in the warm spring breeze

Hex, RGB and CMYK Color Details

	HEX	RGB	CMYK
	#31401A	49,64,26	23,0,59,75
	#8C2E73	140,46,115	0,67,18,45
	#5A5739	90,87,57	0,3,37,65
	#F27405	242,116,5	0,52,98,5
	#F2B705	242,183,5	0,24,98,5
	#BCB39E	188,179,158	0,5,16,26

Embroidery Thread Conversion Chart

	DMC 895 Very Dark Hunter Green
	DMC 917 Medium Plum
	DMC 3362 Dark Pine Green
	DMC 740 Tangerine
	DMC 444 Dark Lemon
	DMC 644 Medium Beige Gray

Witness the beauty of nature blooming in this vibrant spring lupine field

Hex, RGB and CMYK Color Details

	HEX	RGB	CMYK
	#2C4001	44,64,1	31,0,98,75
	#594873	89,72,115	23,37,0,55
	#4F7302	79,115,2	31,0,98,55
	#7E72A6	126,114,166	24,31,0,35
	#C2ADB3	194,173,179	0,11,8,24
	#C1D4D9	193,212,217	11,2,0,15

Embroidery Thread Conversion Chart

	DMC 904 — Very Dark Parrot Green
	DMC 327 — Dark Violet
	DMC 906 — Medium Parrot Green
	DMC 209 — Dark Lavender
	DMC 778 — Very Light Antique Mauve
	DMC 3841 — Pale Baby Blue

A colorful, hand-painted Easter eggs

Hex, RGB and CMYK Color Details

	HEX	RGB	CMYK
	#456BB2	69,107,178	61,40,0,30
	#D55F5F	213,95,95	0,55,55,16
	#4F876C	79,135,108	41,0,20,47
	#F09D33	240,157,51	0,35,79,6
	#3CB8DC	60,184,220	73,16,0,14
	#FFED94	255,237,148	0,7,42,0

Embroidery Thread Conversion Chart

	DMC 3746 — Dark Blue Violet
	DMC 892 — Medium Carnation
	DMC 992 — Light Aquamarine
	DMC 742 — Light Tangerine
	DMC 996 — Medium Electric Blue
	DMC 445 — Light Lemon

Spring has come and the garden is blooming with beauty

Hex, RGB and CMYK Color Details

	HEX	RGB	CMYK
	#161A09	22,26,9	15,0,65,90
	#403A13	64,58,19	0,9,70,75
	#D9043D	217,4,61	0,98,72,15
	#C13955	193,57,85	0,70,56,24
	#A48644	164,134,68	0,18,59,36
	#D8AF86	216,175,134	0,19,38,15

Embroidery Thread Conversion Chart

	DMC 934 — Black Avocado Green
	DMC 3051 — Dark Green Gray
	DMC 3801 — Very Dark Melon
	DMC 891 — Dark Carnation
	DMC 370 — Medium Mustard
	DMC 738 — Very Light Tan

The sweet scent of lilacs fills the air

Hex, RGB and CMYK Color Details

	HEX	RGB	CMYK
	#3C3C13	60,60,19	0,0,68,76
	#7C265F	124,38,95	0,69,23,51
	#AC6CA3	172,108,163	0,37,5,33
	#7D892F	125,137,47	9,0,66,46
	#AEBC81	174,188,129	7,0,31,26
	#E8D3CF	232,211,207	0,9,11,9

Embroidery Thread Conversion Chart

	DMC 936 Very Dark Avocado Green
	DMC 917 Medium Plum
	DMC 33 Fuchsia
	DMC 470 Light Avocado Green
	DMC 164 Light Forest Green
	DMC 225 Ultra Very Light Shell Pink

The blooming Japanese quince is an exquisite sight to the eyes

Hex, RGB and CMYK Color Details

	HEX	RGB	CMYK
	#6a6e65	106,110,101	4,0,8,57
	#dc6661	220,102,97	0,54,56,14
	#6aa8c3	106,168,195	46,14,0,24
	#a36b5f	163,107,95	0,34,42,36
	#831417	131,20,23	0,85,82,49
	#6d8d9e	109,141,158	31,11,0,38

Embroidery Thread Conversion Chart

	DMC 501 — Dark Blue Green
	DMC 351 — Coral
	DMC 813 — Light Blue
	DMC 3859 — Light Rosewood
	DMC 321 — Red
	DMC 334 — Medium Baby Blue

This vibrant Iceland poppy shines like a beacon

Hex, RGB and CMYK Color Details

	HEX	RGB	CMYK
	#B04504	176,69,4	0,61,98,31
	#BF3604	191,54,4	0,72,98,25
	#B1740A	177,116,10	0,34,94,31
	#F17604	241,118,4	0,51,98,5
	#F2A516	242,165,22	0,32,91,5
	#EEB529	238,181,41	0,24,83,7

Embroidery Thread Conversion Chart

	DMC 720 Dark Orange Spice
	DMC 608 Bright Orange
	DMC 783 Medium Topaz
	DMC 740 Tangerine
	DMC 972 Deep Canary
	DMC 444 Dark Lemon

This butterfly soars across the velvety petals of the purple daisy

Hex, RGB and CMYK Color Details

	HEX	RGB	CMYK
	#352324	53,35,36	0,34,32,79
	#A63921	166,57,33	0,66,80,35
	#695356	105,83,86	0,21,18,59
	#89689E	137,104,158	13,34,0,38
	#F27D52	242,125,82	0,48,66,5
	#B49796	180,151,150	0,16,17,29

Embroidery Thread Conversion Chart

	DMC 09 Very Dark Cocoa
	DMC 900 Dark Burnt Orange
	DMC 3860 Cocoa
	DMC 553 Violet
	DMC 3340 Medium Apricot
	DMC 452 Medium Shell Gray

A striking field of vibrant tulips

Hex, RGB and CMYK Color Details

	HEX	RGB	CMYK
	#342F21	52,47,33	0,10,37,80
	#F2385A	242,56,90	0,77,63,5
	#B6654C	182,101,76	0,45,58,29
	#F29F05	242,159,5	0,34,98,5
	#969A98	150,154,152	3,0,1,40
	#ADC8D9	173,200,217	20,8,0,15

Embroidery Thread Conversion Chart

	DMC 3021 — Very Dark Brown Gray
	DMC 3801 — Very Dark Melon
	DMC 21 — Light Alizarin
	DMC 972 — Deep Canary
	DMC 03 — Medium Tin
	DMC 827 — Very Light Blue

Admire the beauty of this sakura tree in full bloom and feel its healing energy

Hex, RGB and CMYK Color Details

	HEX	RGB	CMYK
	#342323	52,35,35	0,33,33,80
	#AC8396	172,131,150	0,24,13,33
	#D284A5	210,132,165	0,37,21,18
	#D5D95F	213,217,95	2,0,56,15
	#AFCFE7	175,207,231	24,10,0,9
	#EADBE4	234,219,228	0,6,3,8

Embroidery Thread Conversion Chart

	DMC 09 — Very Dark Cocoa
	DMC 316 — Medium Antique Mauve
	DMC 603 — Cranberry
	DMC 12 — Tender Green
	DMC 3840 — Light Lavender Blue
	DMC 24 — White Lavender

Lady luck just landed on this gorgeous white flower

Hex, RGB and CMYK Color Details

	HEX	RGB	CMYK
	HEX #0C0A08	RGB 12,10,8	CMYK 0,17,33,95
	HEX #8D2A0B	RGB 141,42,11	CMYK 0,70,92,45
	HEX #9DA616	RGB 157,166,22	CMYK 5,0,87,35
	HEX #FCCC1E	RGB 252,204,30	CMYK 0,19,88,1
	HEX #DEDEDA	RGB 222,222,218	CMYK 0,0,2,13
	HEX #FBFBFB	RGB 251,251,251	CMYK 0,0,0,2

Embroidery Thread Conversion Chart

	DMC 310 Black
	DMC 920 Medium Copper
	DMC 907 Light Parrot Green
	DMC 973 Bright Canary
	DMC 762 Very Light Pearl Gray
	DMC B5200 Snow White

A field of color and joy

Hex, RGB and CMYK Color Details

	HEX	RGB	CMYK
	#394915	57,73,21	22,0,71,71
	#176CA9	23,108,169	86,36,0,34
	#CC3961	204,57,97	0,72,52,20
	#BEAC36	190,172,54	0,9,72,25
	#7CA6C7	124,166,199	38,17,0,22
	#D3D8D1	211,216,209	2,0,3,15

Embroidery Thread Conversion Chart

	DMC 3345 Dark Hunter Green
	DMC 798 Dark Delft Blue
	DMC 891 Dark Carnation
	DMC 166 Medium Light Moss Green
	DMC 809 Delft Blue
	DMC 928 Very Light Gray Green

This sweet and vibrant peach shrubby daisybush is the perfect start to a sunny spring

Hex, RGB and CMYK Color Details

	HEX	RGB	CMYK
	#222601	34,38,1	11,0,97,85
	#8A404A	138,64,74	0,54,46,46
	#BF048D	191,4,141	0,98,26,25
	#616512	97,101,18	4,0,82,60
	#F2836B	242,131,107	0,46,56,5
	#D9B504	217,181,4	0,17,98,15

Embroidery Thread Conversion Chart

	DMC 934 Black Avocado Green
	DMC 3722 Medium Shell Pink
	DMC 3607 Light Plum
	DMC 905 Dark Parrot Green
	DMC 3341 Apricot
	DMC 307 Lemon

Get ready for romance with this bright, heart-shaped bouquet

Hex, RGB and CMYK Color Details

	HEX	RGB	CMYK
	HEX #2C1815	RGB 44,24,21	CMYK 0,45,52,83
	HEX #732426	RGB 115,36,38	CMYK 0,69,67,55
	HEX #C03F3E	RGB 192,63,62	CMYK 0,67,68,25
	HEX #18878C	RGB 24,135,140	CMYK 83,4,0,45
	HEX #18D4D5	RGB 24,212,213	CMYK 89,0,0,16
	HEX #B59593	RGB 181,149,147	CMYK 0,18,19,29

Embroidery Thread Conversion Chart

	DMC 3371 Black Brown
	DMC 221 Very Dark Shell Pink
	DMC 351 Coral
	DMC 3810 Dark Turquoise
	DMC 3846 Light Bright Turquoise
	DMC 152 Medium Light Shell Pink

Witnessing the sun dip below the horizon as purple wildflowers bloom at sunset

Hex, RGB and CMYK Color Details

	HEX	RGB	CMYK
	#15300D	21,48,13	56,0,73,81
	#8D1545	141,21,69	0,85,51,45
	#543A82	84,58,130	35,55,0,49
	#3AABD1	58,171,209	72,18,0,18
	#FFD438	255,212,56	0,17,78,0
	#B3A3AC	179,163,172	0,9,4,30

Embroidery Thread Conversion Chart

	DMC 895 Very Dark Hunter Green
	DMC 600 Very Dark Cranberry
	DMC 3837 Ultra Dark Lavender
	DMC 996 Medium Electric Blue
	DMC 307 Lemon
	DMC 3042 Light Antique Violet

A sweet spring bird rests on the bloomy branches of an enchanted tree

Hex, RGB and CMYK Color Details

	HEX	RGB	CMYK
	#655658	101,86,88	0,15,13,60
	#BF3D79	191,61,121	0,68,37,25
	#AFA459	175,164,89	0,6,49,31
	#BDA2A8	189,162,168	0,14,11,26
	#E2D7C8	226,215,200	0,5,12,11
	#F6F5F7	246,245,247	0,1,0,3

Embroidery Thread Conversion Chart

DMC 3860	Cocoa
DMC 3805	Cyclamen Pink
DMC 472	Ultra Light Avocado Green
DMC 3727	Light Antique Mauve
DMC 3866	Ultra Very Light Mocha
DMC B5200	Snow White

A little stroll through the tulip garden just brightened up my day!

Hex, RGB and CMYK Color Details

	HEX	RGB	CMYK
	#404F3B	64,79,59	19,0,25,69
	#82BF45	130,191,69	32,0,64,25
	#F2D022	242,208,34	0,14,86,5
	#91A4A9	145,164,169	14,3,0,34
	#D9CB9F	217,203,159	0,6,27,15
	#D8DDEA	216,221,234	8,6,0,8

Embroidery Thread Conversion Chart

	DMC 520 Dark Fern Green
	DMC 704 Bright Chartreuse
	DMC 307 Lemon
	DMC 932 Light Antique Blue
	DMC 3047 Light Yellow Beige
	DMC 3747 Very Light Blue Violet

This light pink zinnia is a sign of warmer days ahead

Hex, RGB and CMYK Color Details

	HEX	RGB	CMYK
	#536A5E	83,106,94	22,0,11,58
	#B26556	178,101,86	0,43,52,30
	#748C7C	116,140,124	17,0,11,45
	#FCDD87	252,221,135	0,12,46,1
	#ECB9B4	236,185,180	0,22,24,7
	#B9C0A1	185,192,161	4,0,16,25

Embroidery Thread Conversion Chart

	DMC 501 Dark Blue Green
	DMC 21 Light Alizarin
	DMC 502 Blue Green
	DMC 727 Very Light Topaz
	DMC 761 Light Salmon
	DMC 369 Very Light Pistachio Green

Purple power is taking over!

Hex, RGB and CMYK Color Details

	HEX	RGB	CMYK
	#231C1D	35,28,29	0,20,17,86
	#731D6D	115,29,109	0,75,5,55
	#7429A6	116,41,166	30,75,0,35
	#475537	71,85,55	16,0,35,67
	#7C8C3F	124,140,63	11,0,55,45
	#DFE0DE	223,224,222	0,0,1,12

Embroidery Thread Conversion Chart

	DMC 3799 — Very Dark Pewter Gray
	DMC 34 — Dark Fuchsia
	DMC 3837 — Ultra Dark Lavender
	DMC 520 — Dark Fern Green
	DMC 989 — Forest Green
	DMC 762 — Very Light Pearl Gray

Pink, pretty, and perfect for any occasion!

Hex, RGB and CMYK Color Details

	HEX	RGB	CMYK
	#403740	64,55,64	0,14,0,75
	#6C2A47	108,42,71	0,61,34,58
	#A53061	165,48,97	0,71,41,35
	#D48CAC	212,140,172	0,34,19,17
	#E999B2	233,153,178	0,34,24,9
	#B3C4B6	179,196,182	9,0,7,23

Embroidery Thread Conversion Chart

	DMC 09 Very Dark Cocoa
	DMC 3803 Dark Mauve
	DMC 601 Dark Cranberry
	DMC 3806 Light Cyclamen Pink
	DMC 957 Pale Geranium
	DMC 3813 Light Blue Green

Pink, Purple, White... Cosmos always bring color to our world

Hex, RGB and CMYK Color Details

	HEX	RGB	CMYK
	#203213	32,50,19	36,0,62,80
	#7A002E	122,0,46	0,100,62,52
	#465929	70,89,41	21,0,54,65
	#A6322A	166,50,42	0,70,75,35
	#D35D86	211,93,134	0,56,36,17
	#BDB473	189,180,115	0,5,39,26

Embroidery Thread Conversion Chart

	DMC 319 Very Dark Pistachio Green
	DMC 326 Very Dark Rose
	DMC 987 Dark Forest Green
	DMC 350 Medium Coral
	DMC 956 Geranium
	DMC 3348 Light Yellow Green

Spring tea time vibes in the garden

Hex, RGB and CMYK Color Details

	HEX	RGB	CMYK
	#3C4A1E	60,74,30	19,0,59,71
	#5E7135	94,113,53	17,0,53,56
	#F24822	242,72,34	0,70,86,5
	#D9A714	217,167,20	0,23,91,15
	#D9CF43	217,207,67	0,5,69,15
	#D3CDB8	211,205,184	0,3,13,17

Embroidery Thread Conversion Chart

	DMC 3051 — Dark Green Gray
	DMC 988 — Medium Forest Green
	DMC 947 — Burnt Orange
	DMC 728 — Topaz
	DMC 12 — Tender Green
	DMC 822 — Light Beige Gray

Walking through a field of sunshine

Hex, RGB and CMYK Color Details

	HEX	RGB	CMYK
	#3E510F	62,81,15	23,0,81,68
	#794412	121,68,18	0,44,85,53
	#ECA900	236,169,0	0,28,100,7
	#FFEF03	255,239,3	0,6,99,0
	#BFD16D	191,209,109	9,0,48,18
	#B1D1D5	177,209,213	17,2,0,16

Embroidery Thread Conversion Chart

	DMC 904 Very Dark Parrot Green
	DMC 434 Light Brown
	DMC 972 Deep Canary
	DMC 307 Lemon
	DMC 16 Light Chartreuse
	DMC 3761 Light Sky Blue

Vacay mode: on

Hex, RGB and CMYK Color Details

	HEX	RGB	CMYK
	#253025	37,48,37	23,0,23,81
	#7E4821	126,72,33	0,43,74,51
	#385F65	56,95,101	45,6,0,60
	#568D99	86,141,153	44,8,0,40
	#82B5C5	130,181,197	34,8,0,23
	#C5D8DF	197,216,223	12,3,0,13

Embroidery Thread Conversion Chart

	DMC 500 Very Dark Blue Green
	DMC 434 Light Brown
	DMC 3768 Dark Gray Green
	DMC 518 Light Wedgwood
	DMC 519 Sky Blue
	DMC 3841 Pale Baby Blue

Find your happy place in this breathtaking haven

Hex, RGB and CMYK Color Details

	HEX	RGB	CMYK
	HEX #183C68	**RGB** 24,60,104	**CMYK** 77,42,0,59
	HEX #918881	**RGB** 145,136,129	**CMYK** 0,6,11,43
	HEX #38C3F8	**RGB** 56,195,248	**CMYK** 77,21,0,3
	HEX #90BAE6	**RGB** 144,186,230	**CMYK** 37,19,0,10
	HEX #E8DEC5	**RGB** 232,222,197	**CMYK** 0,4,15,9
	HEX #DDECF5	**RGB** 221,236,245	**CMYK** 10,4,0,4

Embroidery Thread Conversion Chart

	DMC 824 Very Dark Blue
	DMC 3861 Light Cocoa
	DMC 996 Medium Electric Blue
	DMC 809 Delft Blue
	DMC 712 Cream
	DMC 162 Ultra Very Light Blue

There's nothing like watching the sun kiss the ocean at the end of a perfect beach day

Hex, RGB and CMYK Color Details

	HEX	RGB	CMYK
	#464C59	70,76,89	21,15,0,65
	#F27E63	242,126,99	0,48,59,5
	#B28C7F	178,140,127	0,21,29,30
	#F2A766	242,167,102	0,31,58,5
	#A69EA0	166,158,160	0,5,4,35
	#F2E0D0	242,224,208	0,7,14,5

Embroidery Thread Conversion Chart

	DMC 317 Pewter Gray
	DMC 3340 Medium Apricot
	DMC 407 Dark Desert Sand
	DMC 3854 Medium Autumn Gold
	DMC 452 Medium Shell Gray
	DMC 3770 Very Light Tawny

Say 'I do' with sand between your toes

Hex, RGB and CMYK Color Details

	HEX	RGB	CMYK
	#12466D	18,70,109	83,36,0,57
	#4292C6	66,146,198	67,26,0,22
	#68A2C7	104,162,199	48,19,0,22
	#A0A89C	160,168,156	5,0,7,34
	#F5C1C3	245,193,195	0,21,20,4
	#C7D4CD	199,212,205	6,0,3,17

Embroidery Thread Conversion Chart

	DMC 312 — Very Dark Baby Blue
	DMC 3843 — Electric Blue
	DMC 813 — Light Blue
	DMC 927 — Light Gray Green
	DMC 761 — Light Salmon
	DMC 928 — Very Light Gray Green

Nothing beats the serene beauty of a sun-kissed oceanfront

Hex, RGB and CMYK Color Details

	HEX	RGB	CMYK
	#262E2F	38,46,47	19,2,0,82
	#685544	104,85,68	0,18,35,59
	#1D657E	29,101,126	77,20,0,51
	#CB955A	203,149,90	0,27,56,20
	#849399	132,147,153	14,4,0,40
	#E5D3B2	229,211,178	0,8,22,10

Embroidery Thread Conversion Chart

	DMC 3799 Very Dark Pewter Gray
	DMC 08 Dark Driftwood
	DMC 3765 Very Dark Peacock Blue
	DMC 3827 Pale Golden Brown
	DMC 415 Pearl Gray
	DMC 739 Ultra Very Light Tan

Catching some rays while chasing waves

Hex, RGB and CMYK Color Details

	HEX	RGB	CMYK
	#7C583B	124,88,59	0,29,52,51
	#B56C2A	181,108,42	0,40,77,29
	#B88743	184,135,67	0,27,64,28
	#F8C058	248,192,88	0,23,65,3
	#FBC07C	251,192,124	0,24,51,2
	#FEF293	254,242,147	0,5,42,0

Embroidery Thread Conversion Chart

	DMC 3862 Dark Mocha Beige
	DMC 976 Medium Golden Brown
	DMC 729 Medium Old Gold
	DMC 743 Medium Yellow
	DMC 19 Medium Light Autumn Gold
	DMC 445 Light Lemon

Feeling berry good with this cup of blueberries!

Hex, RGB and CMYK Color Details

	HEX	RGB	CMYK
	#364347	54,67,71	24,6,0,72
	#9C4C8D	156,76,141	0,51,10,39
	#7A5F96	122,95,150	19,37,0,41
	#8C8937	140,137,55	0,2,61,45
	#84A0BA	132,160,186	29,14,0,27
	#E4D7DA	228,215,218	0,6,4,11

Embroidery Thread Conversion Chart

	DMC 413 Dark Pewter Gray
	DMC 3607 Light Plum
	DMC 553 Violet
	DMC 471 Very Light Avocado Green
	DMC 794 Light Cornflower Blue
	DMC 24 White Lavender

Sailing into summer with style

Hex, RGB and CMYK Color Details

	HEX	RGB	CMYK
	#3C474E	60,71,78	23,9,0,69
	#497699	73,118,153	52,23,0,40
	#63A5BF	99,165,191	48,14,0,25
	#D9C9A8	217,201,168	0,7,23,15
	#F2DCB3	242,220,179	0,9,26,5
	#EAEDED	234,237,237	1,0,0,7

Embroidery Thread Conversion Chart

	Thread
	DMC 413 — Dark Pewter Gray
	DMC 826 — Medium Blue
	DMC 813 — Light Blue
	DMC 613 — Very Light Drab Brown
	DMC 3047 — Light Yellow Beige
	DMC 3756 — Ultra Very Light Baby Blue

Colorful trio of citrusy goodness

Hex, RGB and CMYK Color Details

	HEX	RGB	CMYK
	#4C3724	76,55,36	0,28,53,70
	#A0182B	160,24,43	0,85,73,37
	#D65E6D	214,94,109	0,56,49,16
	#E9B11C	233,177,28	0,24,88,9
	#D4BC72	212,188,114	0,11,46,17
	#F3D5B9	243,213,185	0,12,24,5

Embroidery Thread Conversion Chart

	DMC 839 — Dark Beige Brown
	DMC 349 — Dark Coral
	DMC 892 — Medium Carnation
	DMC 444 — Dark Lemon
	DMC 165 — Very Light Moss Green
	DMC 951 — Light Tawny

Escape to the picturesque Koze Cafe on Karpathos Island, Greece

Hex, RGB and CMYK Color Details

	HEX	RGB	CMYK
	#3F2817	63,40,23	0,37,63,75
	#935232	147,82,50	0,44,66,42
	#4F615C	79,97,92	19,0,5,62
	#CC815A	204,129,90	0,37,56,20
	#929482	146,148,130	1,0,12,42
	#DFBB94	223,187,148	0,16,34,13

Embroidery Thread Conversion Chart

	DMC 3031 — Very Dark Mocha Brown
	DMC 3826 — Golden Brown
	DMC 501 — Dark Blue Green
	DMC 402 — Very Light Mahogany
	DMC 647 — Medium Beaver Gray
	DMC 738 — Very Light Tan

Let your wanderlust guide you to the enchanting land of Cinque Terre, Italy

Hex, RGB and CMYK Color Details

	HEX	RGB	CMYK
	#465902	70,89,2	21,0,98,65
	#645847	100,88,71	0,12,29,61
	#C13955	193,57,85	0,70,56,24
	#AE8346	174,131,70	0,25,60,32
	#F78545	247,133,69	0,46,72,3
	#A7C8F2	167,200,242	31,17,0,5

Embroidery Thread Conversion Chart

	DMC 905	Dark Parrot Green
	DMC 645	Very Dark Beaver Gray
	DMC 891	Dark Carnation
	DMC 3828	Hazelnut Brown
	DMC 721	Medium Orange Spice
	DMC 3840	Light Lavender Blue

Summertime calls for a berry-licious scoop of heaven

Hex, RGB and CMYK Color Details

	HEX	RGB	CMYK
	#5F0D11	95,13,17	0,86,82,63
	#B62E3B	182,46,59	0,75,68,29
	#B56C2A	181,108,42	0,40,77,29
	#C7718A	199,113,138	0,43,31,22
	#FD839A	253,131,154	0,48,39,1
	#C49EA9	196,158,169	0,19,14,23

Embroidery Thread Conversion Chart

	DMC 3777 Very Dark Terra Cotta
	DMC 3801 Very Dark Melon
	DMC 976 Medium Golden Brown
	DMC 899 Medium Rose
	DMC 3706 Medium Melon
	DMC 3727 Light Antique Mauve

Life is better at the beach and even better with a van by your side!

Hex, RGB and CMYK Color Details

	HEX	RGB	CMYK
	#28243E	40,36,62	35,42,0,76
	#5F5C4B	95,92,75	0,3,21,63
	#5E97C5	94,151,197	52,23,0,23
	#9DA57F	157,165,127	5,0,23,35
	#A6BEC4	166,190,196	15,3,0,23
	#CBCCB3	203,204,179	0,0,12,20

Embroidery Thread Conversion Chart

	DMC 29 Eggplant
	DMC 645 Very Dark Beaver Gray
	DMC 3839 Medium Lavender Blue
	DMC 368 Light Pistachio Green
	DMC 3752 Very Light Antique Blue
	DMC 613 Very Light Drab Brown

The sun is shining and the drinks are flowing!

Hex, RGB and CMYK Color Details

	HEX	RGB	CMYK
	#2E4353	46,67,83	45,19,0,67
	#3E510F	62,81,15	23,0,81,68
	#6E7E40	110,126,64	13,0,49,51
	#B9A216	185,162,22	0,12,88,27
	#CDE4E3	205,228,227	10,0,0,11
	#E2DFE1	226,223,225	0,1,0,11

Embroidery Thread Conversion Chart

	DMC 930 Dark Antique Blue
	DMC 904 Very Dark Parrot Green
	DMC 988 Medium Forest Green
	DMC 166 Medium Light Moss Green
	DMC 747 Very Light Sky Blue
	DMC 27 White Violet

Get ready to feel refreshed with the ultimate poolside pick-me-up!

Hex, RGB and CMYK Color Details

	HEX	RGB	CMYK
	#7E0018	126,0,24	0,100,81,51
	#AE0D13	174,13,19	0,93,89,32
	#EE8700	238,135,0	0,43,100,7
	#3AABD1	58,171,209	72,18,0,18
	#38C4D3	56,196,211	73,7,0,17
	#A1BDCD	161,189,205	21,8,0,20

Embroidery Thread Conversion Chart

	DMC 321 Red
	DMC 606 Bright Orange-Red
	DMC 741 Medium Tangerine
	DMC 996 Medium Electric Blue
	DMC 3846 Light Bright Turquoise
	DMC 3325 Light Baby Blue

When life gives you lemons...take a closer look to see the beauty in every detail

Hex, RGB and CMYK Color Details

	HEX	RGB	CMYK
	#DDAB46	221,171,70	0,23,68,13
	#FFD438	255,212,56	0,17,78,0
	#D0B57E	208,181,126	0,13,39,18
	#DEAD9E	222,173,158	0,22,29,13
	#E7B6AF	231,182,175	0,21,24,9
	#E1CEA3	225,206,163	0,8,28,12

Embroidery Thread Conversion Chart

	DMC 3821 — Straw
	DMC 307 — Lemon
	DMC 3046 — Medium Yellow Beige
	DMC 3779 — Very Light Rosewood
	DMC 761 — Light Salmon
	DMC 3047 — Light Yellow Beige

Chefchaouen, Morocco's charming blue pearl

Hex, RGB and CMYK Color Details

	HEX	RGB	CMYK
	#26659A	38,101,154	75,34,0,40
	#865E6A	134,94,106	0,30,21,47
	#7E97B8	126,151,184	32,18,0,28
	#DCA09E	220,160,158	0,27,28,14
	#B7C7DD	183,199,221	17,10,0,13
	#E4E8ED	228,232,237	4,2,0,7

Embroidery Thread Conversion Chart

	DMC 798 Dark Delft Blue
	DMC 3726 Dark Antique Mauve
	DMC 156 Medium Light Blue Violet
	DMC 3354 Light Dusty Rose
	DMC 800 Pale Delft Blue
	DMC 27 White Violet

Breakfast just got better with a view like this!

Hex, RGB and CMYK Color Details

	HEX	RGB	CMYK
	#2F261A	47,38,26	0,19,45,82
	#A53061	165,48,97	0,71,41,35
	#536A5E	83,106,94	22,0,11,58
	#B0A89B	176,168,155	0,5,12,31
	#B1D1D5	177,209,213	17,2,0,16
	#E5DBCF	229,219,207	0,4,10,10

Embroidery Thread Conversion Chart

	DMC 3021 — Very Dark Brown Gray
	DMC 601 — Dark Cranberry
	DMC 501 — Dark Blue Green
	DMC 648 — Light Beaver Gray
	DMC 3761 — Light Sky Blue
	DMC 3866 — Ultra Very Light Mocha

Even the palm tree knows how to strike a pose for that perfect sunset shot

Hex, RGB and CMYK Color Details

	HEX	RGB	CMYK
	#251B1C	37,27,28	0,27,24,85
	#543A82	84,58,130	35,55,0,49
	#6E3E49	110,62,73	0,44,34,57
	#9C4C8D	156,76,141	0,51,10,39
	#B1475D	177,71,93	0,60,47,31
	#E597AA	229,151,170	0,34,26,10

Embroidery Thread Conversion Chart

	DMC 3799 Very Dark Pewter Gray
	DMC 3837 Ultra Dark Lavender
	DMC 315 Medium Dark Antique Mauve
	DMC 3607 Light Plum
	DMC 3832 Medium Raspberry
	DMC 894 Very Light Carnation

We shell-abrate this beautiful summer day

Hex, RGB and CMYK Color Details

	HEX	RGB	CMYK
	#402D1C	64,45,28	0,30,56,75
	#A65132	166,81,50	0,51,70,35
	#8C3F23	140,63,35	0,55,75,45
	#4C3621	76,54,33	0,29,57,70
	#815C3E	129,92,62	0,29,52,49
	#D4C3AA	212,195,170	0,8,20,17

Embroidery Thread Conversion Chart

	DMC 3031 Very Dark Mocha Brown
	DMC 921 Copper
	DMC 920 Medium Copper
	DMC 3781 Dark Mocha Brown
	DMC 3862 Dark Mocha Beige
	DMC 3033 Very Light Mocha Brown

Cool down from the heat with this tasty watermelon & lime fresh cocktail

Hex, RGB and CMYK Color Details

	HEX	RGB	CMYK
	#526528	82,101,40	19,0,60,60
	#AF7F43	175,127,67	0,27,62,31
	#F07D6E	240,125,110	0,48,54,6
	#71C0A0	113,192,160	41,0,17,25
	#DBBEA8	219,190,168	0,13,23,14
	#E6E8E7	230,232,231	1,0,0,9

Embroidery Thread Conversion Chart

	DMC	Name
	DMC 3346	Hunter Green
	DMC 729	Medium Old Gold
	DMC 3341	Apricot
	DMC 959	Medium Seagreen
	DMC 950	Light Desert Sand
	DMC 3756	Ultra Very Light Baby Blue

Coconut dreams on a sandy beach

Hex, RGB and CMYK Color Details

	HEX	RGB	CMYK
	#252119	37,33,25	0,11,32,85
	#59422E	89,66,46	0,26,48,65
	#916A42	145,106,66	0,27,54,43
	#D97904	217,121,4	0,44,98,15
	#D9A679	217,166,121	0,24,44,15
	#E2E0D7	226,224,215	0,1,5,11

Embroidery Thread Conversion Chart

	DMC 3021 Very Dark Brown Gray
	DMC 08 Dark Driftwood
	DMC 167 Very Dark Yellow Beige
	DMC 741 Medium Tangerine
	DMC 437 Light Tan
	DMC 762 Very Light Pearl Gray

There's something special about waking up early to catch a stunning sunrise over the ocean

Hex, RGB and CMYK Color Details

	HEX	RGB	CMYK
	#4A2748	74,39,72	0,47,3,71
	#6C2A47	108,42,71	0,61,34,58
	#BA8198	186,129,152	0,31,18,27
	#E2A6BE	226,166,190	0,27,16,11
	#F6AA97	246,170,151	0,31,39,4
	#EDD2BF	237,210,191	0,11,19,7

Embroidery Thread Conversion Chart

	DMC 3834 — Dark Grape
	DMC 3803 — Dark Mauve
	DMC 3688 — Medium Mauve
	DMC 604 — Light Cranberry
	DMC 3824 — Light Apricot
	DMC 948 — Very Light Peach

Chasing sunsets is always worth the climb

Hex, RGB and CMYK Color Details

	HEX	RGB	CMYK
	#080101	8,1,1	0,88,88,97
	#80341E	128,52,30	0,59,77,50
	#BE603D	190,96,61	0,49,68,25
	#E48F56	228,143,86	0,37,62,11
	#F4D688	244,214,136	0,12,44,4
	#FDF7DF	253,247,223	0,2,12,1

Embroidery Thread Conversion Chart

	DMC 310 Black
	DMC 918 Dark Red Copper
	DMC 922 Light Copper
	DMC 722 Light Orange Spice
	DMC 727 Very Light Topaz
	DMC 746 Off White

Made in the USA
Las Vegas, NV
03 March 2024

86628114R00057